THE DAY FORT SUMTER WAS FIRED ON

A Photo History
of the Civil War

by Jim Haskins

SCHOLASTIC INC.

New York   Toronto   London   Auckland   Sydney

Acknowledgments

I am grateful to Ann Kalkhoff and Kathy Benson for their help.
Special thanks to my editor, Ann Reit.

To Margaret Emily

Book design: Doug Klein
Photo research by Joan Beard

ISBN 0-590-46397-7

12 11 10 9 8 7 6 5 4 3 2 1   5 6 7 8 9/9 0/0

Printed in the U.S.A.   14
First Scholastic printing, March 1995

TABLE OF CONTENTS

The Civil War began on April 12, 1861, with the attack on Fort Sumter.

THE GUNS OF WAR

Fort Sumter stood on a man-made granite island in the harbor of Charleston, South Carolina. When completed, it was designed to hold 650 soldiers and 146 big guns and was slated to take over, from the older Fort Moultrie a mile or so away, the responsibility of protecting Charleston. In late 1860, Sumter was not yet finished, and workmen were still completing the interior. But already the government of South Carolina was pressing the Federal government to cede it to the state. In December 1860, following the election of Republican Abraham Lincoln to the presidency, South Carolina had seceded from the Union rather than risk losing its status as a slave state.

The commander of the United States garrison at Charleston was a Kentuckian named Major Robert Anderson. Although he was a southerner by birth, and a former

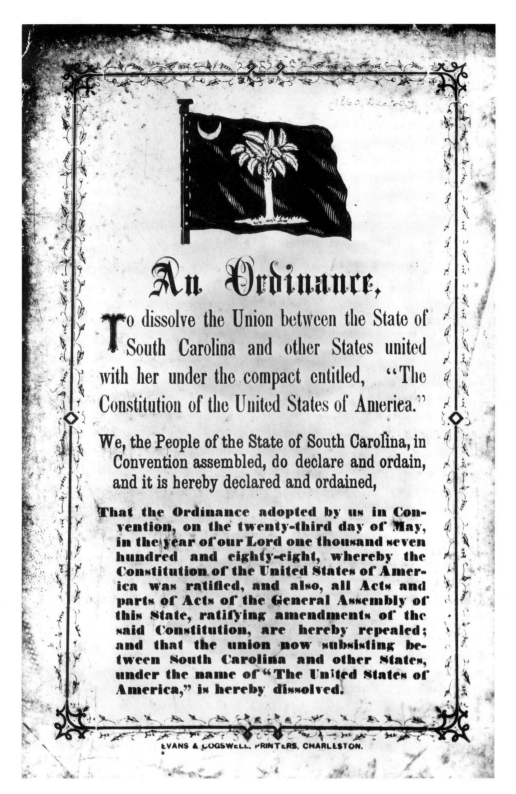

An ordinance to dissolve the Union between the state of South Carolina and the other states

slaveowner, he had served the flag for many years and hated the idea of a divided nation. He asked the Federal government to reinforce his small garrison of about eighty soldiers.

In late 1860, the Federal government was headed by James A. Buchanan, but he was a lame duck president. Buchanan was just serving out his term until Lincoln was inaugurated in early March 1861. He did not wish to take any action that would stir the brewing pot of war. Ceding the Federal forts in Charleston to South Carolina would anger northerners; rein- forcing the Charleston garrison would infuriate southerners. No, Buchanan decided to let the new president worry about what to do.

By the time Abraham Lincoln took the oath of office as the sixteenth president of the United States on March 4, 1861, the United States of America were no longer united. Between December 1860 and February 1861, seven southern states (South Carolina, Georgia, Florida, Alabama, Mississippi, Louisiana, and Texas) had seceded from the Union and formed the Confederate States of

Lincoln's inauguration on the steps of the Capitol, Washington, D.C., March 4, 1861

America. They had also elected a president, Jefferson Davis.

War clouds were on the horizon, but many in the North and South did not want to see armed conflict. Confederates were concerned that the new Confederacy was not organized. Many northerners were afraid that if the president sought to reinforce the Union presence at Charleston, the eight slaveholding states of the upper South that had not seceded would be driven into the Confederacy.

But as the weeks went by, the uncertainty of the situation became dangerous in itself. Both President Lincoln and Confederate President Jefferson Davis were under great pressure to do something.

Meanwhile, at Fort Sumter, Major Anderson and his men had just about run out of food and supplies. This situation gave President Lincoln an idea. He would notify South Carolina Governor Francis Pickens that the Federal government was sending a relief fleet with provisions only. If the Confederates attacked the boats carrying food, they would have to bear the blame for starting a war. This would unite the North and, hopefully, cause divisions in the South.

The fate of the nation now lay in the hands of Confederate President Jefferson Davis. After consultation with his cabinet in Montgomery, Alabama, capital of the Confederacy, he ordered General Pierre G. T. Beauregard to take the fort before the relief fleet arrived.

Thus Beauregard, a West Point graduate who had fought for the Union in the Mexican War (1846–1848), sent a surrender summons to Anderson, also a graduate

Major Robert Anderson, who defended Fort Sumter against the attack led by General Beauregard

of West Point who had fought beside Beauregard in the Mexican War. Anderson refused, and in the early morning of April 12, 1861, Beauregard ordered his Charleston shore batteries to fire on the fort. On April 14, after sustaining thirty-three hours of bombardment that damaged the fort and set the interior on fire, but took no human lives, Anderson surrendered. The Union Stars and Stripes came down; the Confederate Stars and Bars went up. The Civil War had begun.

*Samuel Harper and his wife were two survivors of a group of slaves
freed by the abolitionist John Brown in 1858.*

THE SEEDS OF DISUNION

The seeds of the Civil War
had been planted even before the United
States had been formed. They are contained in the United States Constitution,
which nowhere includes the words *slave* or
slavery. When the Constitution was being
written, slavery was already the backbone
of the southern economy, so its absence
from the document is no accident. It is
absent from the Constitution because the
states could not agree on the question of
slavery, and northern delegates chose to
compromise with their southern counterparts in order to create a *United* States at
the cost of the rights and freedoms of the
Africans and African Americans within the
borders of those states.

Slaves were not the only residents of
the states disregarded in the Constitution.
That document also made no mention of
women, indentured servants, those with-

out property, religious minorities, and ethnic minorities, including the Native Americans from whom the European colonists had seized the land. But all those other groups at least had some basic rights. The slaves had none at all.

The compromises made by the framers of the Constitution led to some odd language: Slaves were referred to as "persons owing service or labor." The compromises also led to some odd mathematics: Southerners insisted that slaves be counted as three-fifths of a man when apportioning representation in the House of Representatives. And these compromises proved to be only the first of many that had to be made to preserve the Union. The question of slave states versus free states arose every time a new state was admitted to the Union.

There were three major compromises in the nineteenth century. The first was the Missouri Compromise of 1820, under which Missouri was admitted to the Union as a slave state and Maine as a free state. The United States was then made up of twenty-four states, half slave and half free.

The second great compromise was the

This five-year-old girl, Fannie Virginia Casseopia Lawrence, was a freed slave who was baptized in 1863 by Henry Ward Beecher, the clergyman and antislavery leader.

John Brown led a raid on Harper's Ferry, Virginia, and was hanged on December 2, 1859.

Compromise of 1850, whereby California was admitted as a free state; other territories were organized without mention of slavery; and a new fugitive slave law was passed.

This new fugitive slave law was aimed at the growing number of slaves, largely from the border states, who were escaping to the North and freedom, and at the people, primarily northerners, who were helping them. Beginning around 1830, Quakers, abolitionists, and other people who were against slavery organized networks to help escaped slaves, by hiding them, feeding them, or transporting them. By the 1840s, these networks were being called the Underground Railroad.

The Underground Railroad was never as large or as well organized as slaveholders said it was. But they used its existence as a reason to push for fugitive slave laws that provided punishment both for the escaped slaves and for those who helped them. Under these laws, aiding an escaped slave was a federal crime. But many free states maintained their right to control what happened within their own borders and insisted that state laws guaranteeing fugitive slaves certain rights outweighed any federal laws to the contrary. So volatile was the slavery issue that the nation was like a powder keg ready to explode.

In Christiana, a small village in Pennsylvania, in September 1851, armed black men protecting two fugitive slaves killed a slaveowner, intent on getting back his property, and wounded his son. A Lancaster, Pennsylvania, newspaper carried the headline: "Civil War: The First Blow Struck." But there was no civil war.

The third great compromise was the 1854 Kansas–Nebraska Act, which provided that Kansas and Nebraska be organized as territories and that their territorial legislatures should decide on the question of slavery. But for that compromise to work,

pro- and antislavery forces had to obey the law of the land, and they did not. Both groups seemed to regard Kansas as a territory they must control at all costs, including the shedding of blood.

In 1856 a mob of some 800 Missourians destroyed the town of Lawrence, Kansas, because the territorial government, many of whose members lived in Lawrence, voted for Kansas to be a free state when admitted to the Union. When he learned of the destruction of Lawrence, John Brown, a Kansan who lived near Pottawatomie Creek, was so incensed that he demanded retribution. With the help of several of his sons and a few other men, he abducted five proslavery settlers and murdered them.

"Bleeding Kansas," as the newspapers referred to the territory, had literally become a battleground in the fight over slavery. Many newspapers referred to "The Civil War in Kansas."

A letter to John Brown from the abolitionist, Frederick Douglass, inviting him to visit

UNCLE TOM'S CABIN AND THE DRED SCOTT DECISION

Two events galvanized the opposite sides in the fight over slavery almost as radically as the battles in Kansas. One was the publication in 1852 of the book *Uncle Tom's Cabin* by Harriet Beecher Stowe. A work of fiction, it dramatized the evils of slavery and the destruction of families by slavery. It persuaded many northerners to join the antislavery crusade. It infuriated southerners, who called Stowe a fanatic and her book "poison."

The other was the U.S. Supreme Court's decision in the case of *Scott* v. *Sandford*. Dred Scott was a Missouri slave whose master had taken him to live first in free Illinois and then in the Wisconsin Territory, where slavery had been excluded under the Missouri Compromise of 1820. After Scott was taken back to Missouri, he sued his master, claiming that living on free soil had made him free. But the majority of the Supreme Court justices disagreed, ruling in 1857 that Scott was not a citizen and thus had no right to bring suit in the courts.

Harriet Beecher Stowe wrote a second novel about the evils of slavery based on that case. Entitled *Dred*, it was not the bestseller *Uncle Tom's Cabin* had been. But no novel was needed to arouse antislavery forces, who were infuriated by the Supreme Court's

Harriet Beecher Stowe, who wrote Uncle Tom's Cabin *in 1852*

300 DOLLARS
REWARD!

RUNAWAY from John S. Doak on the 21st inst., two NEGRO MEN; LOGAN 45 years of age, bald-headed, one or more crooked fingers; DAN 21 years old, six feet high. Both black.

I will pay ONE HUNDRED DOLLARS for the apprehension and delivery of LOGAN, or to have him confined so that I can get him.

I will also pay TWO HUNDRED DOLLARS for the apprehension of DAN, or to have him confined so that I can get him.

JOHN S. DOAKE.

Springfield, Mo., April 24th, 1857,

A flyer offering a reward for two runaway slaves

A drawing of the famous Dred Scott

failure to accord any rights to slaves.

The former fugitive slave and hardworking abolitionist Frederick Douglass hailed the Dred Scott decision for just that reason: "We, the abolitionists and colored people, should meet this decision, unlooked for and monstrous as it appears, in a cheerful spirit. This very attempt to blot out forever the hopes of an enslaved people may be one necessary link in the chain of events preparatory to the complete overthrow of the whole slave system."

Harriet Scott, Dred Scott's wife

A portrait of Abraham Lincoln, taken in Springfield, Illinois, in 1860, before he was elected president

THE BIRTH OF THE REPUBLICAN PARTY

Indeed, the primary reason why the Republican party was formed was to fight slavery. Its founders were abolitionists from several political parties, including Whigs, Democrats, and Free Soilers.

There had been abolitionist parties before, but none had attracted widespread support. By 1854, when the Republican party was officially formed, abolition sentiment in the North was running high, and by the election of 1856, the new party was a force to be reckoned with.

By 1860, Republicans believed they had a real chance at winning the White House. They chose as their candidate a lawyer from Illinois named Abraham Lincoln. Lincoln, who had spent his political life as a member of the Whig party, was relatively unknown on the national scene,

A political cartoon depicting the Lincoln-Douglas debates during the 1858 senate campaign

having served just one term in Congress (1847–49) and having lost his bid for the Senate in 1855. After joining the Republican party in 1856, his moderate views on slavery and his gift for oratory helped him to rise rapidly in the ranks of the organization.

In 1858, the Republicans nominated him to oppose the Democrat Stephen A. Douglas for the Illinois Senate. Lincoln challenged Douglas to a series of debates, which became famous for setting forth the differences over slavery. In fact, slavery was the only subject of all seven debates. Although Douglas won the election, Lincoln had made his mark as a man who could articulate the moderate Republican philosophy. Two years later, he was the Republican presidential candidate, and in November 1860, he was elected to the nation's highest office. He received a minority of the popular vote, but the Democratic party had split its vote, and as a result Lincoln got more votes than any other candidate.

Lincoln's and the Republican party's antislavery position was poison in the South, and his election was the signal for secession. South Carolina left the Union in December 1860, and by the time of Lincoln's inauguration on March 4, 1861, six more southern states had followed South Carolina's lead.

PATRIOTS, NORTH AND SOUTH

The action at Fort Sumter opened the floodgates of emotion in both the North and the South. Each side had been frustrated by the lack of action before the capture of the fort. Now, both were eager to fight for their side. On April 15, President Lincoln issued a call for 75,000 militiamen to "maintain the honor, the integrity, and the existence of our National Union." The free states of the North answered with patriotic zeal. At war meetings throughout the region, people cheered the flag and vowed vengeance on the southern traitors. Even in places like New York City, where there had previously been a great deal of sympathy for the South, the Confederate action in South

A Union soldier, Corporal J.P. Goodliff, in a photograph taken by Mathew Brady

Carolina was seen as traitorous.

The states of the upper South reacted quite differently to the president's call for help from state militias. Although they had not seceded with the seven states below their borders, they had strong sympathies with the secessionists. Most of these states' governors refused outright to furnish any fighting forces. Maryland and

On a southern plantation, cotton is ginned.

Delaware simply did not reply. The inhabitants of these states realized they had to cast their lot with either the North or the South and that they could no longer occupy a middle ground. By May, four upper South states—Arkansas, North Carolina, Virginia, and Tennessee—had joined the Confederacy. That same month, it was decided to move the capital of the

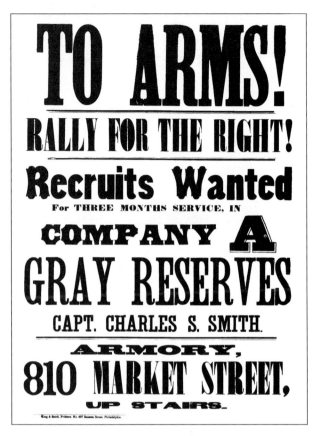

Soldiers enlisted for three months' service, as this recruiting poster shows.

Confederacy from Montgomery, Alabama, to Richmond, Virginia, because of Virginia's greater prestige as one of the original colonies. But Virginia was also much closer to the North, putting the Confederate capital in greater danger.

Three border states that remained in the Union—Maryland, Kentucky, and Missouri—had large populations of southern sympathizers.

In spite of the weaknesses represented by those border states, the Union had a much stronger position than the Confederacy. It represented twenty-three states to the Confederacy's eleven. It had twenty-two million people compared to the South's nine million. Every third south-

A group of Confederate soldiers posed for a Richmond photographer before the Battle of Bull Run, 1861.

erner was a Negro, and the majority of these were slaves. The North had better railroads, more ships, and more factories. It also had a much more diversified economy. With so much in their favor, northerners didn't think the war would last much more than three months.

The South relied almost entirely on one crop—cotton—for its livelihood. Confederate leaders believed cotton was enough, however, for it was much sought after throughout the world, and the South had many ports from which to send it. The South was surrounded by the ocean and the Gulf of Mexico; it was unlikely that the Union Navy could seriously interfere with the international cotton trade; Southerners believed they could withstand whatever the North had to give out in the course of what some had called the "ninety-days' war." Unlike the North, which had to actually win the war, the

Jefferson Davis, President of the Confederacy, with his wife, Varina

South saw its task as merely protecting itself from being conquered.

The South had another advantage, at least in the early years of the war. It had more experienced officers and soldiers than the North. Its president, Jefferson Davis, was a former soldier and secretary of war. The South was able to organize its military much more quickly than the North, and this was evident in the preponderance of Confederate land victories in the first three years of the war.

John Gooseberry was a fife player with Company E of the 54th Massachusetts regiment.

Many children, such as this boy, worked for the soldiers.

THE CHILDREN'S WAR

Neither side understood just what would be involved in waging the War Between the States. Both northerners and southerners were thoroughly convinced that they would be victorious in a short time. Both sides talked about a ninety-days' war, and, in fact, the initial length of army enlistment on each side was ninety days. Farmers calculated that they would be home well before harvest time.

Not only did both sides misjudge the length of the war, they also underestimated the tragedy of the war. Perhaps it was because they would be fighting neighbors, but they failed to understand what guns and bullets, and cannons and cannonballs would do to human beings. This was especially true of civilians, and civilians represented the major manpower of the war effort.

Much of that "manpower" was provid-

Some soldiers brought their families to the front.

ed by children, especially by boys under the age of eighteen. No one knows exactly how many youths fought in the Civil War, but it is estimated that between ten and twenty percent of the fighting forces were underage when they enlisted.

Most young people volunteered because they sought adventure and escape from the boredom of their lives. In the early days of the war, when everyone thought it would be over in a short time, these young people thought it would be fun and exciting to be part of the conflict. Later on, they enlisted with a greater sense of the reality of war and of the hardships they faced. But they still enlisted, out of a sense of patriotism or duty.

It was fairly easy for boys who looked older than their age to enlist. In those days there existed very few proofs of age, such as birth certificates or Social Security cards or drivers' licenses. Army recruiters asked enlistees how old they were and generally accepted the answers. Eighteen was the minimum age for recruits. There was also a height requirement of five feet five inches. A small fifteen-year-old would be questioned, but a tall fifteen-year-old who said he was eighteen would usually be believed.

The easiest way for an underage youth to get into the army was to enlist as a musician, such as a drummer or bugler. One twelve-year-old wrote, "I wanted to fight the Rebs, but I was very small and they would not give me a musket. The next day I was back and the man behind the desk said I looked as if I could hold a drum and if I wanted I could join that way. I did, but I was not happy to change a musket for a stick."

Children were too young to enlist as soldiers, but they could serve as musicians on the battlefield. This boy, Henry Munroe, was a drummer for Company C, 54th Massachusetts regiment, an all-black regiment.

Musicians were considered very important for troop morale. In the course of the war, some 40,000 musicians served in the Union army, and about half that number for the Confederacy. Since musicians were not supposed to engage in combat, recruiters did not concern themselves with the age of a musician-enlistee. So frequently were drummers and buglers underage that the terms *drummer boy* and *bugle boy* were in common use.

The role of the drummer was very important in the war. Drumbeats were ways of communicating to the soldiers, and frequently, amidst thick smoke, it was the only way soldiers could locate their units. Although musicians were not supposed to engage in combat, they were frequently in the thick of fighting. Stories abound of a bugle boy picking up a regimental flag and raising it aloft after the flag carrier had been felled by enemy fire. Nor did enemy bullets discriminate between soldiers and musicians. In fact, in some cases the drummer was a target of enemy fire. Many musicians died in the fighting, and the Civil War was the last time drummer boys were used in battle.

A young Civil War boy in uniform

John Joseph Clem, age 10, was known as the Drummer Boy of Shiloh.

Boys who wanted to do "a man's job" found that there was much more to army life than adventure. They had to drill endlessly in order to be ready to fight. They found out that soldiers spent much more time waiting for orders or marching from one place to another than fighting. They were often harassed by older soldiers and had to prove themselves equal to the men. And when they actually got into battle, they realized it was a scary, serious business.

Elisha Stockwell, Jr., a fifteen-year-old Wisconsin boy, ran away and enlisted over the objections of his family. But he regretted his action when he found himself face-down on the ground, with enemy shells exploding around him: "I want to say, as we lay there and the shells were flying over us, my thoughts went back to my home, and I thought what a foolish boy I was to run away and get into such a mess as I was in. I would have been glad to have seen my father coming after me."

This boy, and other very young soldiers, were not alone in being afraid in battle. Grown men had similar feelings. And there is no question that if they survived the war, no matter how old they were, these boys had become men.

Wounded soldiers wait for treatment at Savage Station, Viginia.

BULL RUN

Neither side was ready for what would prove to be a bloody, long war. In the case of the Confederacy, this was understandable. Although it had in place most of the trappings of a federal government, such as elected officials and a constitution, it did not have the recognition of any foreign government. Confederate leaders had hoped to gain official recognition as a sovereign government from Great Britain, one of the South's major cotton customers, but the British people were opposed to recognizing a government that supported slavery.

The Confederacy had to decide how to share the responsibilities of waging war between the individual states and the new government. The Confederacy had no navy and little or no capability of building one, since the South had so little industry and no shipyards. Its army was a different story. Even though the Confederacy had

LINCOLN'S TWO DIFFICULTIES.

Lin. "WHAT? NO MONEY! NO MEN!"

An 1862 political cartoon from Punch, *a British satire magazine.*

A lithograph by Currier and Ives, depicting the Battle of Bull Run, July 21, 1861

to create a war department and build an army from scratch, there were fine southern generals and dozens of volunteer militia companies filled with southern men who honestly believed they could whip the Yankees. Still, for all their zeal, these soldiers could do only so much. Without sufficient supplies and arms and ammunition, problems getting these materials plagued the South from the beginning.

The Union was as ill-prepared for war in its own way as the secessionist group. Most of its small, 16,000-man army was stationed at frontier outposts in the West, where their main job was fighting Indians and protecting western settlers. Most of the forty-two ships in the navy were patrolling waters thousands of miles away from the United States. But the North had the capacity to build up

General Pierre G.T. Beauregard, the Confederate commander at Manassas, Virginia, the site of the Battle of Bull Run

Union General Irvin McDowell led the attack against General Beauregard's troops.

quickly, which it proceeded to do.

And then there was the question of how to wage war. In 1861 the military colleges, such as West Point, were still teaching methods of combat that had been taught before industrialization. It had long been known that one reason why the American Revolution succeeded was that the British regiments stood up on the battlefields like so many sitting ducks just waiting to be picked off by the colonial guerilla fighters. But the tactics taught at American military schools largely followed the British model. The Union and Confederate commanders stuck to the rules, even though the forces they commanded were overwhelmingly untried volunteers—farmers and shopkeepers, amateurs at war.

Nowhere was this more evident than at Bull Run, a river near Manassas, Virginia. The Union strategy was to try to capture the Confederate capital at Richmond. As part of the "Forward to Richmond" plan, Union General Irvin McDowell set out from Washington to attack the troops of General Pierre G. T. Beauregard. Beauregard, whose attack on Fort Sumter had started the war, was the Confederate commander at Manassas. Meanwhile, Union General Robert Patterson was to set out from the Shenandoah Valley to attack the forces of General Joseph E. Johnston, farther south in the valley.

On the morning of July 21, 1861, McDowell's troops launched their attack on Beauregard's. Both the Union and Confederate soldiers had signed on for ninety-day stints in the armed forces, and their time was almost up. The majority fought bravely in spite of considerable confusion.

In addition to the expected confusion among men not trained to do battle, there was confusion over uniforms and flags. Neither side had a consistent uniform or style of dress, and often it was difficult to tell at whom one was shooting. The same was true of the flags of the two sides—the Union's Stars and Stripes and the Confederacy's Stars and Bars were hard to distinguish in the smoke and haze of battle. After Bull Run, General Beauregard designed a new battle flag, with white stars embedded in a blue cross on a red field.

At first the odds were very much in favor of the Union, with its 10,000 troops against the 4,500 Confederates. But Confederate reinforcements kept coming, including a brigade of Virginians from the Shenandoah Valley commanded by Thomas J. Jackson. Accounts differ about what South Carolina General Barnard Bee said when he saw Jackson arrive, but either admiringly or critically he likened him to a stone wall. Jackson would become one of the Civil War's most famous and best generals, and was forever after known by the nickname "Stonewall."

Although eventually some 18,000 men were aligned on each side, the Union strategy did not include sending in as many reinforcements as did the Confederate plan. By midafternoon many of the Union brigades were tired and fighting in a disconnected fashion. Beauregard saw his opportunity to launch a major counterattack. With a high-pitched scream that later came to be known as the "rebel yell," Confederates swarmed over the Yankees, many of whom panicked and beat a fast retreat. Not all the Union brigades scattered. Some units of General William Tecumseh Sherman's brigade held fast, as did several companies from the Regular Army. They managed to slow the progress of the rebels, whose pursuit was nearly as disorganized as the Yankee retreat.

But disorganized and late as it was, the victory belonged to the Confederates. It was as much a psychological victory as a battlefield one, and the spirit it instilled in the Confederate soldiers helped them go into succeeding battles with a sense that they could win.

Historians of the war now give much credit to the Confederate officers for keeping their men united and pressing forward even in the face of heavy fire. They seemed to understand better than Union officers that it was essential to keep the troops' morale high. For that reason they tolerated, and perhaps even encouraged, the unmilitary but emotionally satisfying "rebel yell," which has been described as a "mingling of Indian whoop and wolf-howl." Another reason why Confederate morale seemed to be higher was that southern strategy was offensive while, except for Bull Run, Union strategy, at least in the early years of the war, was usually defensive.

On the Union side, the defeat instilled a gnawing sense of doubt among northern troops and officers that was difficult to overcome. President Lincoln took steps to overcome it by playing to the Union's strengths. Within three days of Bull Run, he issued orders calling up one million soldiers for three-year enlistments. He also ordered increased efforts to blockade the South's main ports.

Confederate forces continued to be victorious in most of the important land battles of 1861 through early 1862, despite the fact that Union forces managed to capture Nashville, Tennessee, on February 23, making it the first Confederate state capital to fall into Union hands. In acknowledgment of the generally bad news from the West, Confederate President Jefferson Davis chose to be officially inaugurated on February 22, 1862, in a black suit and to say in his inaugural address that "after a series of successes and victories, we have recently met with serious disasters." Still, it was victories by the Union Navy during that same period that had the greater and more lasting effect.

General Robert E. Lee said of General Thomas J. "Stonewall" Jackson (above), "He was the outstanding soldier of the War Between the States."

General Robert E. Lee, on his horse Traveller

THE NAVAL WAR

The Union Navy was substantial, as was the North's capability of manufacturing and outfitting additional naval forces. The fleet quickly succeeded in blockading most of the South's major ports, although Confederate merchant ships and private vessels were often successful in running these blockades. The major drawback for the navy was that the Union had only two bases in the South: Hampton Roads, near Confederate-held Norfolk, Virginia, and Key West, Florida. So, the navy decided to seize additional bases.

In late August 1861, two Confederate-held forts guarding Hatteras Inlet off the coast of North Carolina surrendered rather than face a planned naval onslaught. The following month the Confederate forces guarding half-completed fortifications on Ship Island halfway between Mobile, Alabama, and New Orleans, Louisiana, gave up with hardly a fight after the Union Navy volleyed a few shells at them.

On November 7, after only four hours of fighting, the navy knocked out the two forts guarding Port Royal, South Carolina, and took control of the finest natural harbor on the south Atlantic Coast.

Hoping to stem the tide of Union naval victories, Confederate President Jefferson Davis appointed the Virginian army general Robert E. Lee as commander of the south Atlantic coastal defenses. But Lee could only do so much. There were so many ports and harbors for the navy to attack, and the Confederacy had little in the way of a navy to resist those attacks. During the next several months, the Union seized several other harbors and ports.

In the face of this serious situation, the South built the first ironclad ship, armor-plating the hull of the *Merrimack*, a salvaged frigate, equipping its prow with an iron ram, and arming it with guns and pivot rifles. The resulting creation, which

The sinking of the U.S.S. Cumberland *by the* Merrimack, *March 8, 1862*

was called the *Virginia*, was supposed to be a new kind of naval warcraft, capable of battering through ships that blockaded a harbor. In its first engagement, at the mouth of the James River at Hampton Roads off the coast of Norfolk on March 8, 1862, the *Virginia* managed to sink one Union ship and blow up another, causing navy's own experiment with iron ship-building arrived to confront the *Virginia*. John Ericsson's all-iron *Monitor*, jokingly referred to as a "cheese box on a raft" because of its odd-looking construction, was waiting for the *Virginia* when she steamed out to finish off the Union fleet. The two ships fired at each other for two

Crewmen on deck of the U.S.S. Monitor

240 Union sailors to lose their lives. While she sustained considerable damage, not one of the shots fired at her had penetrated her armor.

But the following morning, the Union hours, neither scoring a decisive hit. But together they had scored another kind of victory: They had proved that ironclads were the wave of the future in naval warfare. But that wave would not appreciably

Admiral David Farragut's fleet at Port Hudson

affect the Civil War. Although the Union built 58 ironclads and the Confederacy 21, the main naval action was still undertaken by the old wooden steam and sailing ships.

Using such ships in early April 1862, the Union navy took control of the entrance to Savannah, Georgia. On April 24, Admiral David Farragut slipped his boats past two forts at the mouth of the Mississippi River, which protected New Orleans. Disregarding his orders to cease his attack after those victories, he then captured the entire city. By the end of that month, along the whole southern Atlantic coast only the harbors at Charleston, South Carolina, and Wilmington, North Carolina, remained free of the Union blockade.

Not only was this situation bad for Confederate morale, it was serious for the well-being of the Confederacy. Goods could neither be sent nor received from blockaded harbors. The South's cotton could not be sent to European ports, and thousands of bales sat idle by quiet docks. European goods could not reach the blockaded ports, causing severe shortages in everything from food to dry goods like shoes to war materials like rifles and gunpowder. Nor could one Confederate state transport goods to another by water. The Union capture of New Orleans meant that the South could no longer bring in supplies from the Gulf of Mexico for its troops in the West.

THE PEOPLE'S WAR

Although there was considerable action in the West, those battles have not gone down in history as equally important with those in the East. One reason was that both Washington, DC, the Union capital, and Richmond, Virginia, the Confederate capital, were located in the East. But another major reason was that the eastern battles received better coverage from the major metropolitan newspapers that reported on the war.

The Civil War was the first war in history to be covered thoroughly by the press. Not only did newspaper correspondents go into the thick of the fighting to render eyewitness accounts, but the newly invented telegraph enabled them to send back their reports so that readers could learn what had happened the very next day. Reporters from northern newspapers

Many newspapers, such as the New York Herald, *sent reporters to the front.*

A U.S. military telegraph battery wagon, near Petersburg, Virginia, in 1864

like the New York *Herald* and New York *World* risked their lives to get their stories, disguising themselves as women or as Confederate soldiers in order to get behind southern troop lines.

They were so thick around the headquarters of Union generals that one general, William Tecumseh Sherman, threatened to shoot them. Other Union generals worried about the security issues the reporters posed. Not unlike the military men who complained that extensive media coverage compromised the United States efforts during Operation Desert Storm against

Newspapers kept people up-to-date on each battle of the war.

Iraq in 1991, the Union generals said that the newspaper correspondents were giving away valuable information. But freedom of the press was an established right. In response to such criticisms, the New York *World* insisted that the Civil War was a "people's war" and that the people had a right to know what was happening.

Because northern newspapers provided the most extensive and widely read coverage of the war, many of the major battles of the war are better known today by the names Union generals gave to them than by those their Confederate counterparts gave to them.

In most cases, the Union forces chose as names the landmark closest to the fighting or to their own lines, while the Confederates named the battle after the town that served as their own base. Thus, the Confederates fought two battles at Manassas, Virginia, while the Union forces fought the same two battles at Bull Run river.

Not only were the people able to read about the events of the war, they were also able to see photographs showing in graphic detail the ravages of the war. Mathew

Brady was a practitioner of this new technology, having opened up his own studio in New York in 1844. He had begun photographing President Lincoln in 1860 and after the war broke out was authorized to accompany and photograph the armies. He organized a photographic corps, which made a huge visual record of the war, the first war to be so thoroughly documented.

Photographers, such as Mathew Brady (far right), supplied a visual record of the Civil War.

The Battle of Shiloh was one of the bloodiest battles of the war.

SHILOH

There was much to document in the Civil War, and no greater opportunity to show the blood and gore of war presented itself than at Shiloh, a Civil War battleground whose name even today resonates with valor and tragedy.

The Confederates usually named their battles after towns. But Shiloh was the name of a small church near the spot of the first Confederate attack. The Union forces named the battle Pittsburg Landing, following their custom of naming a battle after a local landmark. Why in this case the Confederate name of Shiloh stuck is not known, but perhaps the tragic loss of lives in that battle lent itself better to a Biblical name (the original Shiloh was a town northwest of Jerusalem, home of the prophet Eli). Fought by Union forces under the command of generals Ulysses S. Grant and Don Carlos Buell, among others,

General Ulysses S. Grant scored a narrow victory at the Battle of Shiloh.

and by Confederate forces under generals Beauregard and Johnston, among others, this battle over a small area of Tennessee proved to be a harbinger of later battles in its scale of death and injury. The 20,000 deaths and injuries sustained about equally between the two sides were nearly double the deaths and injuries of the major conflicts of the previous year combined. Although the Union forces were victorious in the end, the price paid diminished the sense of victory. On the Confederate side, no matter how close to victory the southern forces had come, serious psychological damage was done—especially given the Union naval victories at Savannah, New Orleans, and elsewhere.

The comparative population statistics of North and South had begun to tell by this time. Faced with the fact that the North had more people, and thus more able-bodied soldiers than the South, Confederate president Jefferson Davis sought, and gained from his Congress on April 16, 1862, the first conscription law in American history. Under this law, all able-bodied white men between the ages of 18 and 35 were required to serve their country for a period of three years.

The Battle of Shiloh was also called the Battle of Pittsburg Landing by Union forces.

44

THE WOMEN'S WAR

As the conscription law attested, the Civil War was a white man's war. Women were not expected to take part, other than to make bandages and knit socks for the troops. But like the underage boys who enlisted anyway, women wanted to play a bigger role than men were willing to allow them, and they did.

A small number of women actually saw battlefield action in the Civil War; they disguised themselves as boys and volunteered for the army. It is impossible to know how many women posed as men, but several dozen were discovered by doctors

Civil War women volunteers

Some women worked for the soldiers, doing their laundry and other chores.

at camp hospitals after being wounded in battle. If several dozen were found out this way, there may have been several hundred women who saw action.

Some went into battle because they could not bear to be separated from their husbands. Although it was not at all uncommon for whole families to go to war, and for women to try to keep a semblance of family life in the camps, some women also chose to fight side by side with their men. They were able to keep their identities secret because soldiers slept in their clothes at night and rarely took baths. The

women ran little risk of exposing their bodies and being discovered.

Amy Clark put on a Confederate uniform to be near her husband, and kept on fighting after he was killed in 1862. Loreta Vasquez begged her husband to take her with him when he joined the Confederate army. He refused, but after he left, she enlisted under the name Harry Buford and even recruited her own battalion.

Other women believed they could fight as well as men. Sarah Edmonds first enlisted in the Union army as a male nurse and later worked as a Union spy. She had

Clara Barton, founder of the American Red Cross

already masqueraded as a man in civilian life. After running away from home to escape an arranged marriage, she took the name Franklin Thompson and worked in a publishing company. After the war, Edmonds married and had three children. Her secret might never have been revealed if she hadn't tried to get a military pension.

There were women attached to the Union army who were known as regimental daughters. They lived in camps and had their own tents. They marched with the soldiers and acted as nurses and helpers. Kady Brownell served as a regimental daughter with three different Rhode Island regiments.

As the war years went on, women played an ever greater role in caring for the many casualties. Before Shiloh, women were not considered professional

Kady Brownell fought beside her husband with the Rhode Island Volunteers, in spite of rules prohibiting women from serving in the Union Army.

Elizabeth Blackwell, the first woman doctor in the United States

caretakers but housewives with a hobby, and their nursing tasks were considered menial work, not a profession. By the time of the Civil War, professional women in the health field were rare. It was only eleven years before the outbreak of war that the first American woman, Elizabeth Blackwell, managed to overcome male prejudice to win an MD (Doctor of Medicine) degree. And only one year before the outbreak of the Civil War did Florence Nightingale in England establish the world's first school of nursing.

While women in both the North and South came forward to offer aid after the Civil War broke out, northern women already had a tradition of public, voluntary service and so made greater strides more quickly in establishing their importance to the war effort. Elizabeth Blackwell spearheaded the drive in the North, organizing a meeting of three thousand women at Cooper Union in New York, out of which came the Women's Central Association for Relief. The WCAR established the first training program for nurses in the United States and later became the basis of the United States Sanitary Commission.

Modeled after the British Sanitary Commission, which was formed to fight unsanitary conditions that bred disease and death among Allied troops during the Crimean War (1853–56), the United States Sanitary Commission functioned as a civilian auxiliary to the Medical Bureau. Its officers and its paid staff were men; but most of its tens of thousands of volunteer workers were women. Its various chapters held "Sanitary Fairs" to raise money and send bandages, food, medicine, clothing, and volunteer nurses to army camps and hospitals. Dorothea Dix, who had built a

Sojourner Truth, an abolutionist who also fought for women's rights

reputation for her work in reforming insane asylums, worked in cooperation with the U.S. Sanitary Commission to recruit nurses.

While the majority of women who served as nurses for the Union troops during the Civil War were volunteers, by war's end some 3,000 women had held positions as paid army nurses.

Harriet Tubman (far left) and seven slaves she helped free. Tubman also served as a scout, laundress, and nurse during the war.

And then there were the women who operated independently of either the armed forces or such organizations as the United States Sanitary Commission, the separate Western Sanitary Commission, and the Christian Commission operated by the Young Men's Christian Association (YMCA). One such woman was Clara Barton, who raised money for medicines and supplies and then traveled to wherever the action was, bringing medical care and comfort to wounded soldiers at several battlefields. Mary Ann Bickerdyke also took it upon herself to follow the Union armies, cleaning up the filthy conditions in the camps and otherwise helping to make the lives of enlisted men better. She traveled with both generals Grant and Sherman and was the only woman that General Sherman allowed in his base camp hospitals.

Still another independent nurse was Harriet Tubman, who had gained fame as a "conductor" on the Underground Railroad before the war broke out. During the war, she made it her business to nurse the escaped slaves who found their way to Union lines. After the war, she tried to obtain a pension from the government for her services but was unsuccessful.

It is said that southern women were behind many of the eager Confederate soldiers who had volunteered to fight when the war first broke out. Legend has it that these women insisted that their men fight to preserve slavery and the southern way of life because slaveowning white women stood to lose the most if slavery and the southern way of life were to end.

Southern women were less accustomed to activity of any sort outside the home, and the percentage of southern women who were active in the war effort was smaller than that of northern women. There was no Sanitary Commission in the South. Still, many southern women flouted convention and volunteered to care for the sick.

In Richmond, Virginia, Sally Louisa Tompkins founded her own infirmary and was later commissioned a captain by President Jefferson Davis so that her infirmary could qualify as an army hospital. By September 1862, the Confederate Congress had authorized the use of civilians in army hospitals and passed a law that gave "preference in all cases to females where their services may best serve the purpose."

In addition to rendering valuable service to the war effort by caring for the sick, many northern and southern women found new self-respect, not to mention new respect from their men. The war was a long and bloody one, and most Americans were changed by it in one way or another.

Families visit soldiers in a convalescent camp in Alexandria, Virginia.

THE PENINSULA CAMPAIGN

Union General George B. McClellan, commander of the Peninsula Campaign, photographed with his wife

One of the most strategic regions in the Civil War was the peninsula of land surrounded by the Chesapeake Bay, the Potomac River, and the James River. It contained Richmond, capital of the Confederacy, and President Lincoln believed that controlling the peninsula was crucial to winning the war. He urged General George B. McClellan to present a plan to take the peninsula, and in the spring of 1862, the general finally launched a campaign that he hoped would end in the capture of Richmond.

McClellan, however, consistently over-estimated Confederate troop strength and hesitated to attack at times that Lincoln thought were ripe. McClellan also concentrated on attacking *places* while Lincoln would have preferred that he attack *armies*. Confederate troops were able to retreat in the face of the superior Union force, which displeased Confederate President Jefferson Davis but which kept the Confederate forces intact. In retreating, Confederate forces commanded by General Joseph E. Johnston, left the port city of Norfolk, Virginia, exposed. It was captured by Union forces on May 10, 1862.

At one point, McClellan's army approached to within six miles of Richmond. This scandalized the Confederacy. Reports of Confederate defeats in the West were no boost to morale. Jefferson

An encampment of the Army of the Potomac at Cumberland Landing

Davis was desperate to do something to turn the tide of the war. Davis had come to rely more and more on General Robert E. Lee. In late June, he ordered Lee to launch a campaign to control the strategic peninsula.

Armed with fresh recruits garnered as a result of the new conscription law, Lee led attacks on Union forces for seven days between June 25 and July 1, 1862, in a series of confrontations that came to be known as the Seven Days' Battles. While the Confederacy won no decisive victories, Lee's carefully planned campaign resulted in a strategic victory, because the Union forces consistently retreated once they had forced the rebels back. But both sides paid a terrible price. The 30,000 men killed and wounded equaled the number of casualties in all previous battles during the first half of 1862. The Seven Days' Battles established a new pattern for hard fighting and severe casualties.

Not all the casualties were military in nature. Sickness also took its toll in the Peninsula Campaign. It seriously affected the strength of Union General George B. McClellan's troops. Nearly a quarter of his men were sick with malaria, dysentery, and typhoid, and the worst months of the year for sickness—August and September—were yet to come. Because of the ailing and weakened state of McClellan's troops, President Lincoln ordered the general to withdraw from the peninsula. McClellan protested, feeling that even burdened by sickness, his troops could accomplish the limited objective of capturing the Confederate capital of Richmond.

When McClellan's forces withdrew, the Confederacy rejoiced, believing that the end of the war, and a Confederate victory, were at hand. But just the opposite end had been assured. As Civil War historian James M. McPherson has explained, "If McClellan's campaign had succeeded, the war might have ended. The Union probably would have been restored with minimal destruction in the South. Slavery would have survived in only slightly modified form, at least for a time. By defeating McClellan, Lee assured a prolongation of the war until it destroyed slavery, the Old South, and nearly everything the Confederacy was fighting for."

The ward of an Army hospital in Washington, D.C.

A skirmish between the Brooklyn 14th and rebel cavalrymen at Antietam

ANTIETAM AND THE EMANCIPATION PROCLAMATION

Now President Lincoln's objectives had changed. Before, he had hoped to preserve the Union with a minimum of damage. Now, he understood that he would have to defeat the Confederacy. For his part, Confederate President Jefferson Davis also dug in his heels and sought to attack Union territory. In September, General Lee attempted to invade Maryland, setting the stage for the battle of Antietam (Sharpsburg).

The fighting at Antietam was among the hardest of the war, and the casualties were the worst. More than twice as many Americans, northerners and southerners,

Dead soldiers in front of Dunker Church on the Antietam battlefield in 1862

fell in one day in that battle than had fallen in the War of 1812, the Mexican War, and would fall in the future Spanish-American War *combined.*

Five days after Antietam, President Lincoln called his cabinet together and announced that he had made a promise to God that if the Union army drove the Confederates from Maryland, he would issue the Emancipation Proclamation. He needed to issue the proclamation after a victory in order for it to have the greatest psychological effect.

The Emancipation Proclamation freed all slaves in the Confederacy as of January 1, 1863. Lincoln had been thinking about issuing it at least since July. He considered it an important military tactic. Slaves were Confederate property, and since the Union was at war with the Confederacy, he had the right as Commander in Chief of the Union forces to order the seizure of enemy property.

Some abolitionists scoffed that Lincoln had freed the slaves in areas where he had no power and that he had allowed all those in areas he did control to remain in slavery. But the president had no constitutional right to act against slavery in areas loyal to the Union.

The final Emancipation Proclamation President Lincoln signed on New Year's Day, 1863, contained a further provision—black soldiers and sailors were to be

A northern poster depicts the promised freedom and education for black people.

allowed to enlist in the Union forces.

Free blacks had wanted to enlist in the Union army since the war had broken out, but they had been refused. In the eyes of the War Department, the Civil War was a "white man's war." Besides, there was no tradition of black enlistment. Although blacks had served in the Revolutionary War and in the War of 1812, the Regular Army had never admitted black soldiers. Even state militias had been all-white since 1792.

The Navy had been less prejudiced and had accepted blacks from the beginning, mainly as firemen, coal heavers, and stewards. But blacks had also served as gunners, and Robert Smalls, a former South Carolina slave who had

President Lincoln and General McClellan at Antietam, October 3, 1862

Robert Smalls was hailed a hero when, as a crewmember, he steered the Confederate gunboat The Planter *into Union territory.*

escaped to the Union fleet blockading Charleston harbor, was now a Union navy pilot.

The main reason for deciding to enlist blacks was a practical one. It was felt that black soldiers could serve in labor battalions, thus freeing white soldiers for combat. But in reality, blacks served in combat roles as well as support roles, right from the beginning.

THE NEGROES' WAR

There were four-and-one-half million blacks in the United States when the Civil War began. The vast majority of them lived in slavery in the South. All of them had a keen interest and major stake in the outcome of the war, yet whites on both sides tried to keep them out of it.

One of the primary reasons for secession was that the Confederate states wished to preserve "southern institutions," chief among them slavery. The Confederacy fought to preserve slavery for a year-and-a-half (between the attack on Fort Sumter and Lincoln's issuance of the Emancipation Proclamation) before the Union finally sought outright to fight to abolish slavery.

From the beginning of the fighting, blacks had made significant contributions to the war effort on both sides. In the early years, both slaves and free blacks

Freed black laborers on a wharf at the James River

Officers at Fifth Army corps headquarters at Harrison's Landing, James River, Virginia

were of invaluable help to the Confederacy. Some free blacks formed companies and volunteered their services to Confederate officials. In some cases, their offer of help was accepted and they were employed as labor battalions to build fortifications. In the main, these men were motivated by a desire to show that they could be patriotic and by the hope that they might earn better treatment as a result.

Frequently, individual slaves accompanied their masters to war to serve them on the battlefield and in the field camps, just as they had served them at home. While some did so unwillingly, others were eager to make their masters' lives easier, for they either liked their masters or believed so firmly that it was their Christian duty to serve that they did not question this duty even in war. Considering the difference in total population between the North

and the South, the work of southern slaves was invaluable to the Confederate war effort, for their performance in labor battalions freed up whites for combat.

But many southern slaves and free people of color saw the outbreak of war as a chance to escape their condition. Especially in border areas, slaves made their way to the Union lines as fast as they

ty used "in aide of the rebellion." Since most of the slave "contrabands" had in some way aided the Confederacy, whether by growing food or building fortifications, this confiscation act covered essentially all the escapees.

Even in the Deep South, far away from the Union troops, some slaves took advantage of the unsettled times to escape, and

Men of the First New York Engineers and members of the 54th Massachusetts regiment worked together to build barriers against rebel fire at Fort Wagner.

could. There they were accepted as "contraband," or illegal goods. By the end of July 1861, General Benjamin Butler had 900 "contrabands" at his camp near New Orleans, Louisiana. By early August, the U.S. Congress had passed a "confiscation act" providing for the seizure of all proper-

many owners deliberately moved their slaves to areas far away from population centers in an attempt to forestall mass desertions. By the end of the war, some 500,000 slaves had escaped to Union lines.

In the North, black abolitionists like Frederick Douglass pressed the Federal

Many black soldiers, such as Company E of the 4th United States Colored Infantry, saw battle.

government to allow black enlistment. Douglass, and many other blacks, slave and free, northern and southern, believed the Civil War was about slavery and thus about black people in America. They wanted to be part of the action. But Lincoln was concerned that making slavery the main issue in the war would be a mistake. Many northerners were against abolition and fearful of the idea of thousands of free Negroes. Many southerners who had mixed feelings about their region's secession would support the Confederacy without question if the main issue was slavery.

But as the conflict wore on, it seemed inevitable that slavery should become the main issue and its abolition one of the primary aims of the Union. And once the abolition of slavery became a chief aim, it followed that blacks should be allowed to take part in the fight.

Even before the Emancipation Proclamation was issued, black regiments had been organized in Kansas and Louisiana, as well as in South Carolina, and Governor John Andrew of Massachusetts was eager to do the same in

Colonel Robert Gould Shaw, commanding officer of the 54th Massachusetts Regiment

his state. In a short time, with the help of prominent abolitionists, Andrew had enlisted two regiments of black men from northern states: the 54th and 55th Massachusetts.

The 54th Massachusetts would become the most famous black regiment in the Civil War. In the early evening of July 18, 1863, the 54th, after a forced march that had lasted a day and a half, attacked Fort Wagner, a Confederate fortification guarding the entrance to Charleston Harbor. The Confederates answered with a murderous volley of gunfire. The regiment's young white colonel, Robert Shaw, was killed at the head of his regiment, but his men fought on. White regiments were supposed to come in to support the 54th, but none came, and without such support the regiment finally had to retreat. Frederick Douglass's son, Lewis, was one of the lucky survivors.

Although the 54th's assault on Fort Wagner was a failure (because it did not accomplish its goal of capturing the fort), it successfully proved the bravery of black troops under fire and their willingness to die for the Union cause. After the war ended, the New York *Tribune* looked back on the Fort Wagner assault as a milestone

Martin R. Delany, a physician who became the first black field officer in the Union Army

in the war: "It is not too much to say that if this Massachusetts Fifty-fourth had faltered when its trial came, two hundred thousand colored troops for whom it was a pioneer would never have been put into the field. ... But it did not falter. It made Fort Wagner such a name to the colored race as Bunker Hill has been for ninety years to the white Yankees."

More than 200,000 blacks fought in the Union army and navy. Without them, the North could not have won the war as soon as it did.

The 1st Battalion of the 13th United States Infantry fighting at Vicksburg, Mississipi, May 19, 1863

VICKSBURG AND GETTYSBURG

The age of modern warfare was ushered in during the Civil War. This was partly because of the development of modern technology. It was also due to the shrewdness and abilities of two Union generals, Grant and Sherman.

The Civil War was the first war in which the railroad, steamship, and electric telegraph played an important role. There had been no new developments in weaponry when the war broke out, but the war speeded their development. Breech-loading rifles came into use, with their increased range of effectiveness.

The existence of railroads was especially crucial to the change in the way warfare was conducted. While the North had a larger network of railroads and thus could move its troops and supplies more efficiently within its own territory, Union efforts to push southward during 1862 and 1863 were blocked or paralyzed by Confederate cavalry

Many Union soldiers lost their lives at the Battle of Gettysburg.

Alfred R. Waud, an artist, sketching the battle at Gettysburg

raids on rail lines of supply.

That is what happened when General Ulysses S. Grant tried to move on Vicksburg, Mississippi, in late 1862. Confederate General Nathan Bedford Forrest managed to outfox and outfight several Union regiments while destroying fifty miles of railroad and telegraph lines as well as great quantities of equipment. Finding himself deep in enemy territory without a supply line, Grant was forced to retreat to Tennessee. During the retreat, Grant's army lived off the food they found along the way, and Grant was amazed at how much food there was.

The following spring, Grant made another try at Vicksburg. In a campaign that lasted from April to July, Grant, along with generals William Tecumseh Sherman, James McPherson, and John McClernand, moved to cut off the area by making a wide circuit eastward and then northward. In so doing, the Union forces cut loose from their own supply lines for a short time, but Grant knew they could live off the land in the meantime. By May 7, they managed to cut Vicksburg's line of supply and reinforcement, and six weeks later the

Confederate garrison at Vicksburg was starved into surrendering. Vicksburg fell to the Union forces on July 4, 1863, a humiliating date, considering that it was the anniversary of Independence Day.

With control of Vicksburg came control of the Mississippi River. Meanwhile, in Pennsylvania in early July, Confederate troops were forced to beat a retreat from Gettysburg. It was not a good summer for the Stars and Bars. These two campaigns proved to be the crucial turning point in the war.

The Gettysburg campaign was espe-cially costly to both sides. Twenty-three thousand Union soldiers were killed, wounded, or missing-in-action. The cost to the Confederacy was some five thousand higher. President Lincoln declared the battlefield a national cemetery. It was offi-cially dedicated on November 19, 1863.

Many dignitaries made speeches at the dedication, some of them especially long-winded. President Lincoln's remarks were distinguished by their brevity, and by the powerful commitment to the Union they expressed. Lincoln's Gettysburg Address is one of the most famous and often quoted

Countless children lost their fathers during the war. This picture was found in the hands of a soldier who lay dead on the battlefield of Gettysburg.

Lietenant Van Pelt (center) defending his battery at the Battle of Chickamauga

speeches in history. The written speech reads in part:

> Four score and seven years ago our fathers brought forth on this continent, a new nation, conceived in liberty and dedicated to the proposition that all men are created equal. Now we are engaged in a great civil war, testing whether that nation, or any nation so conceived and so dedicated, can long endure. . . .we here highly resolve that these dead shall not have died in vain—that this nation, under God, shall have a new birth of freedom—and that government of the people, by the people, for the people, shall not perish from the earth.

There was still hope for the Confederacy. In the fall, the South enjoyed victory at Chickamauga and succeeded in keeping Union forces at bay at Chattanooga. Well into 1864 the Union troops failed to capitalize on their previous successes, much to the dismay of the northern people. Unrest and disillusionment over the war were so great that President Lincoln feared he would not be reelected that November. Many people, certain that the war was not winnable by the North, wanted a president who would negotiate peace with the Confederacy, even if it meant the end of the Union. The Democratic party nominated George B. McClellan, Lincoln's former supreme commander, as their presidential candidate. McClellan had always favored a negotiated peace, even when he was responsible for the Union's military strategy. Only a decisive victory would save the presidency for Abraham Lincoln.

SHERMAN'S MARCH

General William Tecumseh Sherman provided that victory.

With his prospects for winning the 1864 election in doubt, Lincoln made changes in his military. He made General Ulysses S. Grant supreme commander of the Union armies and ordered him to take Richmond. Grant, however, was unable to accomplish this mission. His armies drew close to Richmond but were unsuccessful in routing the Confederates.

Meanwhile, Sherman succeeded to Grant's former position as commander of the western forces. He devised a bold

General William Tecumseh Sherman at Atlanta, Georgia

Soldiers on Sherman's "March to the Sea," carrying their laundry as it dries, May 15, 1864

strategy to capture Atlanta, Georgia, the junction of four important railroads, a crucial source of supplies for Confederate troops in the western theater, and, as Sherman himself noted, "full of foundries, arsenals, and machine shops." Sherman recognized that as one of the largest cities in the South, Atlanta's fall would deal a severe psychological blow to the Confederacy.

What caused that strategy to work was Sherman's understanding of what had paralyzed earlier Union efforts: the reduction of mobility provided by the railroads. The new technology, which enabled supplies and troops to be moved more quickly and efficiently, had allowed commanders not only to build up increased numbers of troops but also to count on more supplies for those troops. But in doing so, they had created cumbersome, demanding armies that could not move quickly.

Starting from Chattanooga, Tennessee, Sherman was 330 miles from Louisville, Kentucky, his main line of supplies. But Sherman had already taken steps to be less dependent on that line of supplies. Every man was ordered to

carry five days' rations. No tents were allowed, except for the sick or wounded. Each regiment was allowed only one wagon and one ambulance. Without the burden of stocks of supplies, Sherman's army was able to move quickly.

Between the first of May and the end of August, Sherman's forces destroyed the railroads and cut off the roads leading to Atlanta from both North and South. On

September 1, the Confederates were forced to evacuate.

Northerners went wild with rejoicing. President Lincoln now enjoyed the position of victorious leader, and his reelection

The capture of Atlanta, Georgia, by the Union Army, under General Sherman, 1864

Union soldiers destroyed railroad tracks leading to Atlanta, Georgia, cutting off supplies and troops to the Confederate Army.

ceased to be in serious doubt. He beat McClellan by an overwhelming margin. Southerners despaired. In many ways, Atlanta symbolized the South. Now it was in Union hands.

Sherman did not stop with his victory over Atlanta. He determined to "march to the sea," driving eastward through Georgia, wrecking its railway system and stopping the northward flow of supplies to Richmond. Once again, Sherman abandoned his own line of supply, moving with a minimum of transport and living off the farms and towns through which he traveled, all the while destroying the railroads.

Starting from Atlanta in mid-November, he reached the Atlantic port of Savannah, Georgia, in just four weeks.

Confederates sank into even greater despair. There seemed no stopping Sherman. His destruction of crucial southern railroads and supply lines did on land what the Union naval blockade had done at sea—cut off supplies and starved the Confederacy. But what it did to the southern spirit was almost worse. As Confederate General E.P. Alexander wrote, "the moral effect of this march...was greater than would have been the most decided victory."

President Lincoln entering Richmond, Virginia, the former capital of the Confederacy, April 3, 1865

THE FALL OF RICHMOND

By early 1865, the feeling on both sides was that the war would be over soon. In his second inaugural address, President Lincoln spoke of a new country that would arise from the ashes of the South and gave promise of a forgiving attitude on the part of the Federal govern-ment when he used the words, "With malice toward none; with charity for all."

In the South there was a sense of helplessness and a lack of will to continue. General Grant finally bestirred his troops around Richmond and Petersburg to resume their advance on Richmond. Success was quick and dramatic. General Robert E. Lee's army was headed off and forced to surrender within a week.

Jefferson Davis, President of the Confederate States of America, had to leave his capitol, and once he did, there was a mass exodus as citizens used every means of conveyance to get out of town. On April 3, 1865, the Confederate flag atop the capitol came down and the Stars and Stripes of the Union were raised high.

That same day, the President of the United States entered the former capital of the Confederacy. Abraham Lincoln had wanted to be present at the end, which he had known would come soon. With an escort of only ten sailors, Lincoln walked through the streets of Richmond. Presidential aides were concerned about

The city of Richmond, Virginia, in ruins in April, 1865

the risk of assassination. But they needn't have worried. As historian James M. McPherson has written, "the Emancipator was soon surrounded by an impenetrable cordon of black people shouting 'Glory to God! Glory! Glory! Glory!'. . . Overwhelmed by rare emotions, Lincoln said to one black man who fell on his knees in front of him: 'Don't kneel to me. That is not right. You must kneel to God only, and thank Him for the liberty you will enjoy hereafter.'"

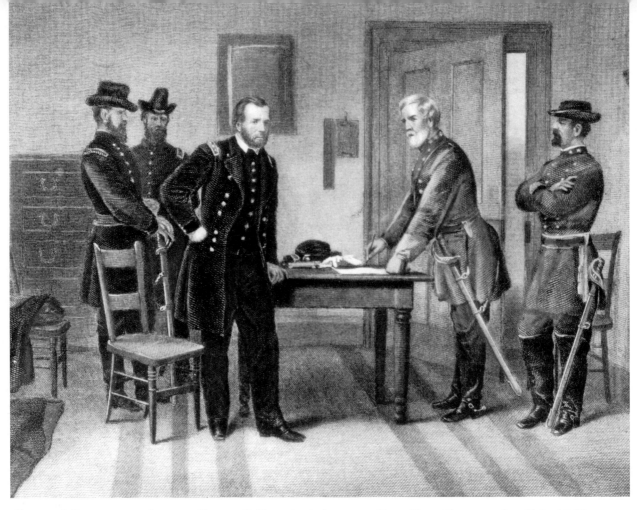

General Lee surrenders to General Grant at Appomattox Courthouse, April 9, 1865.

The scattered remains of General Lee's army rendezvoused at Amelia Courthouse thirty-five miles to the west. They had hoped to find food; but there was only ammunition. So it was necessary to scour the countryside for food, and the delay proved fatal. Lee had intended to follow the railroad down to Danville, where Jefferson Davis was trying to rally the Confederacy and where Lee hoped to join with the troops of General Joseph E. Johnston. But Union General Philip Sheridan cut off the railroad to Danville, forcing Lee to change direction toward Lynchburg.

On April 6, pursuing Union forces cut off about 9,000 men, a quarter of Lee's remaining army, capturing 6,000 of them. The following day, General Grant called on Lee to surrender. Desperate, Lee tried a breakout attack against Sheridan's troops blocking the road near Appomattox Courthouse. Soon realizing he was surrounded by Union forces, Lee sent a note of surrender to Grant.

In the parlor of the home of one Wilmer McLean, the two generals went through the formalities. After the papers were signed, Grant introduced Lee to his staff. As he shook hands with Grant's military secretary, Ely Parker, a Seneca Indian, Lee stared at Parker and said, "I am glad to see one real American here." Parker responded, "We are all Americans."

Pen and ink sketch of the scene at Appomattox Courthouse with General Lee and his adjutant

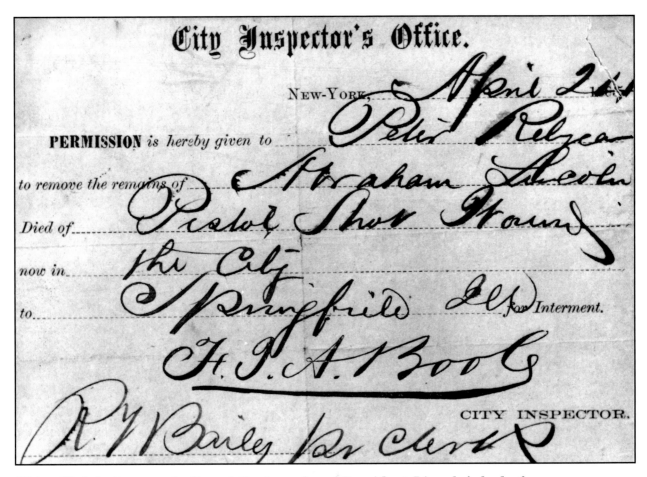

This official city record allowed the transfer of President Lincoln's body from Washington, D.C., to Springfield, Illinois, for burial.

RECONSTRUCTION AND ITS AFTERMATH

Four years of fierce fighting had produced 500,000 dead, either on the battlefield or in hospitals, prisons, and camps. Close to 300,000 people were wounded. It had also resulted in the occupation of the seven defeated Confederate states by Union troops. Politically, these states were in a no-man's-land.

Abraham Lincoln's major concern all along had been the preservation of the Union, and he believed that the sooner the errant states were welcomed back to the Union, the sooner the Union would be fully restored. He had already set his plan in motion through his treatment of Confederate states that Union troops had conquered earlier, such as Louisiana, Arkansas, and Tennessee. In each case, he had allowed those states considerable freedom, asking in exchange only that they pledge allegiance to the Union. His

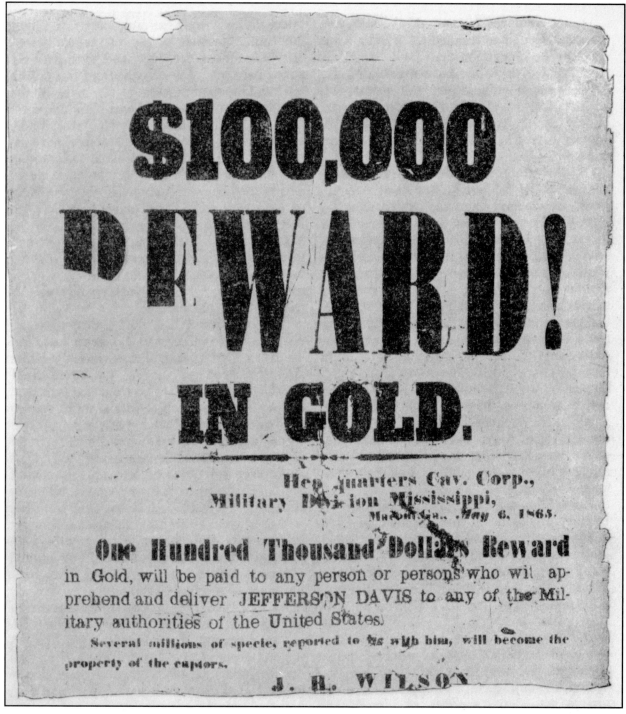

This poster offers a reward of $100,000 for Jefferson Davis.

method was to gently show them the way.

In the case of Louisiana, for instance, as he had said in a speech on April 11, he would have preferred the state to have given the vote to literate Negroes and black veterans and hoped it would soon do so. But even this gentle persuasion was hateful to diehard defenders of slavery. On hearing Lincoln's speech, the actor John Wilkes Booth declared, "That means nigger citizenship. Now, by God, I'll put him through [put a bullet through him]. That is the last speech he will ever make."

Four days later, on April 15, 1865, Booth shot Lincoln as he sat in the presidential box at Ford's Theater in Washington, DC. The president died the following morning.

In the wake of Lincoln's assassination, President Andrew Johnson (Lincoln's vice president who had succeeded to the presidency), attempted to carry out the slain president's program. But many in the former rebel states did not consider the program that became known as Presidential Reconstruction at all generous. Resentful of their conquerors, and especially of the former slaves, they were determined to restrict the lives of the freedmen and return to the old ways as quickly as possible.

By the end of 1865, many localities had instituted laws aimed at keeping blacks virtual slaves. These Black Codes included laws that made all blacks prove that they were employed, or face arrest; that made disrespect to an employer by a black a crime; that prevented blacks from even renting real estate.

In response, Congress, which was controlled by the Republican party, passed a civil rights bill on the one-year anniver-

Ku Klux Klan members, wearing hoods to hide their identities, burn a cross as a warning of impending violence.

The Fifteenth Amendment granted black men the right to vote for the first time.

sary of General Lee's surrender. This bill aimed to guarantee the rights of the freedmen.

When southern white racists could not accomplish their aims through laws, they turned to lawlessness, and there were many incidents of white violence against blacks. The Ku Klux Klan, founded in Tennessee in 1865, began as a social club but soon became an organization with chapters throughout the South that was devoted to doing violence to blacks and their white friends.

Further angered, a branch of the Republican party known as the Radicals passed, over President Johnson's veto, the Reconstruction Act of 1867, ushering in what was called Radical Reconstruction.

Under the Reconstruction Act, any white southerner who had directly aided the Confederate cause was denied the vote, and that effectively meant most white southern men (women could not vote in those days). Blacks, including former slaves, were given full citizenship and so had the opportunity to vote and hold office, and to participate in the writing of new state constitutions.

In many former Confederate states, the Reconstruction governments were made up of whites—northerners and southerners—and blacks, primarily in the lower houses of the state legislatures. They passed forward-looking laws and wrote highly democratic constitutions that called for universal public education, a greatly expanded electorate, and many other provisions, including the rebuilding of the southern economy, that would benefit everyone. They were remarkably forgiving of former diehard slavery advocates.

But the vast majority of white southerners deeply resented the Reconstruction governments. As a result, when northerners grew tired of the disruptions caused by the war and the twelve years of Reconstruction, Federal troops were pulled out. Bitter southerners immediately took steps to undo everything that had been foisted upon them during Reconstruction. At the top of their list was rescinding nearly every right the freedmen had enjoyed for that brief time.

Meanwhile, the freedmen had not been well prepared for freedom. Although some attempts had been made, primarily through the Freedman's Bureau of the Federal government, to educate and resettle former slaves, they had not been provided with the wherewithal to make the most of freedom. Many slaves believed that they would be given forty acres and a mule after the war was over. But this proved to be an empty hope. Without land or the means to make a living, the former slaves were easy prey for the southern whites who blamed the slaves in large measure for causing the war.

Through successive segregation laws, the post-Reconstruction southern governments made sure that Negroes would have less education, less health care, and essentially no political rights. It would be almost a full century between the outbreak of the Civil War to the start of the civil rights movement that eventually guaranteed the rights of full citizenship to blacks in the South.

A freed black man and woman at Savannah, Georgia, in 1875

In the aftermath of the civil rights movement, a so-called New South arose— a South where blacks and whites, who had always lived in close proximity with each other, learned to respect one another; a South in which blacks believed there were greater opportunities than in the supposedly more liberal North. Today Atlanta, once the symbol of the Confederacy, stands as the symbol of the New South, with a black mayor, an annual Black Expo, and special trade relationships with several African nations. In 1988 Virginia, once the capital of the Confederacy, became the first state in the Union to elect a black governor, L. Douglas Wilder.

Nevertheless, bitterness over the war still lingers in the South, where some state capitals still fly the Confederate flag and where some racist groups display the Stars and Bars along with the Nazi swastika. Most towns have statues of Confederate soldiers, and in some areas children are practically grown before they learn that the South *did not* win the war. As Abraham Lincoln understood, the Civil War was the greatest threat to the Union in its history, and slavery the most divisive issue. If he were alive today, he probably would not be surprised at the fact that economic and racial injustice continue to divide the people of our nation.

IMPORTANT DATES, 1820–1877

1820
Missouri Compromise enacted

1850
Compromise of 1850 passed

1854
Kansas–Nebraska Act passed

1860
November—Republican Abraham Lincoln elected sixteenth president of the United States

December 20—South Carolina secedes from the Union, followed soon after by Mississippi, Florida, Alabama, Georgia, Louisiana, and Texas

1861
February 4—Delegates from the secessionist states, except Texas, whose representatives were delayed, meet in Montgomery, Alabama, and form the Confederate States of America

February 9—Jefferson Davis of Mississippi and Alexander Stephens of Georgia are elected president and vice president of the Confederacy

March 4—Abraham Lincoln inaugurated president

March 11—Representatives of the new Confederate States of America adopt a constitution containing states' rights provisions and recognizing and protecting slavery

April 12–13—Confederate general P.G.T. Beauregard orders the bombardment of Fort Sumter from the Charleston, SC, shore batteries; Major Robert Anderson surrenders the fort

May—Arkansas, North Carolina, Virginia, and Tennessee join the Confederacy; the capital of the Confederacy is moved from Montgomery, AL, to Richmond, VA

July 21—First Battle of Bull Run (Manassas)

1862
February 22—Jefferson Davis officially inaugurated as president of the Confederate States of America

February 23—Confederate forces evacuate Nashville, TN, making it the first Confederate state capital to fall to the Union

April 6–7—Battle of Shiloh (Pittsburg Landing)

April 26—Union Navy Admiral David G. Farragut captures New Orleans
June 25–July 1—The Seven Days' Battles

August 29–30—Second Battle of Bull Run (Manassas)

September 17—Battle of Antietam (Sharpsburg)

December—Union decides to accept Negroes into its armed forces

1863
January 1—President Lincoln signs the Emancipation Proclamation freeing all slaves in the Confederacy

April–July—Battle of Vicksburg

July 1–3—Battle of Gettysburg

May 7—Union General William Tecumseh Sherman begins his march toward Atlanta, GA

September 1—Atlanta falls to the Union

November—President Lincoln is reelected

November 19—Lincoln delivers the Gettysburg Address

November–December—Sherman's "March to the Sea"

1865
April 3—Richmond, VA, falls to the Union

April 9—General Lee surrenders to General Grant at Appomattox, VA

April 15—Lincoln assassinated by John Wilkes Booth

1866
April 9—On the first anniversary of Lee's surrender, Congress passes a Civil Rights Act designed to protect Negroes from Black Codes and other discriminatory efforts in the South

1867
March 2—Congress enacts the first Reconstruction Act

1868
July 28—Fourteenth Amendment to the Constitution, declaring all persons born or naturalized in the United States are citizens and entitled to the equal protection of it's laws

1870
March 30—Fifteenth Amendment to the Constitution, guaranteeing blacks the right to vote, is ratified

1877
Reconstruction officially ends when newly elected president, Rutherford B. Hayes, orders the withdrawal of all Federal troops from the former Confederacy

FOR FURTHER READING/VIEWING

YOUNG READERS

Angle, Paul M., ed. *A Pictorial History of the Civil War Years.* New York: Doubleday, 1967

Burns, Ken. *The Civil War.* PBS Videos, 1989

Chang, Ina. *A Separate Battle: Women and the Civil War.* New York: Lodestar, 1991

Cosner, Shaaron. *War Nurses.* New York: Walker, 1988

Katz, William Loren. *Reconstruction and National Growth 1865–1900.* New York: Franklin Watts, Inc., 1974

Murphy, Jim. *The Boys' War: Confederate and Union Soldiers Talk About the Civil War.* New York: Scholastic, Inc. 1990

Ray, Delia. *A Nation Torn: The Story of How the Civil War Began.* New York: Lodestar, 1990

Ray, Delia. *Behind the Blue and Gray: The Soldier's Life in the Civil War.* New York: Lodestar, 1991

YOUNG-ADULT READERS

Angle, Paul M., ed. *A Pictorial History of the Civil War Years.* New York: Doubleday, 1967

Burns, Ken. *The Civil War.* PBS Videos, 1989

Cox, Clinton. *Undying Glory: The Story of the Massachusetts 54th Regiment.* New York: Scholastic Inc., 1991

Foner, Eric. *Reconstruction: America's Unfinished Revolution, 1863–1877.* New York: Harper & Row, 1988

Haskins, Jim. *Get on Board: The Story of the Underground Railroad.* New York: Scholastic Inc., 1992

McKissack, Patricia and Fredrick. *Ain't I A Woman? The Story of Sojourner Truth.* New York: Scholastic Inc., 1992

INDEX

Page references in italics indicate material in illustrations or photographs.

PHOTO CREDITS